For

Mose --

I feel this book has great relevance for you but only because of the name & the Texas part -- not because I expect you to wind up in prison or anything and maybe you don't even know anyone named Gracie. Anyway I hope it doesn't really suck.

Have a great summer!

Kathy

Mose

Loren Graham

Wesleyan University Press

Published by University Press of New England
Hanover and London

Wesleyan University Press
Published by University Press of New England
Hanover, NH 03755
© 1994 by Loren Graham
5 4 3 2 1
CIP data appear at the end of the book

ACKNOWLEDGMENTS

Cover illustration: Max Beckmann, *Falling Man*. Gift
of Mrs. Max Beckmann. © 1994 National Gallery of
Art, Washington.

Days 1741–1722 and 1643–1639 of this poem were
published previously, in slightly different form, in
Timbuktu 6 (Spring 1991).

Days 1623–1619 appeared previously under the
title "Mose and Mail Call" in *Lilt* 2 (Fall 1992).

My thanks to Greg, Kent, and Charles for their
good help at the critical moments.

for my parents

for Ann

Mose

1741

Dear Gracie do you hate me for it

Mose smashes the yellow legal page
into a ball and reaches for the dead

cigarette, whose smoke still lingers, clings
on his hair and the bars of his cell
and the one light bulb in its wire cage—

Mose Peterson, bewildered in the Texas
Department of Corrections, lost in the letter
to the woman whose face swirls in his mind

on the long days while the heels of his hands
harden on a shovel handle, and the sun darkens
his neck and the back of his white uniform—

He stares at the sunburn on the top of his arm
and waits, thinking how the lights go out
precisely at ten and without regard:
                                        He begins again

Listen Gracie I just wanted

Look Gracie I won't bother

Dear Gracie I

1740

Whistle of brakes in the peanut field: Mose
in white cotton, last name stencilled
in black over shirt pocket and hip

pocket, stands in the crosshatches of shadow
the dawn makes through the steel mesh windows
of the whitewashed, crackerbox schoolbus,

slips the smokes he rolled on the way
into the Camel pack in his front pocket,
comes at last to the door and the impossible

breadth of central Texas, the scarlet
lip of its horizon, the big trusty
like a tower on the back of the roan

stallion, bullwhip coiled in his fist,
the riflemen across the gravel road
shading their faces with the brims

of cowboy hats, Mose's mind
muttering *Dear Gracie Dear*
Gracie

1729

Dear Gracie I can't talk to you
on some things. There ain't no use
to try and explain. It's just how

The darkness comes suddenly, as always,
and Mose lies down with his thoughts
as always: alone among criminals, himself

criminal, feeling that suits him
like a hand-me-down except when he remembers
the blackness that descended on him unexpected

when guilt rose to hang like a celestial stranger
watching over his shoulder. He draws
a long breath, closes his eyes, and sees

himself, a small boy throwing the switch,
trying to leap into bed before the light was gone.
"The dark is fast," he says in a whisper

into the same black-lettered white
pillow that alone hears when Mose laughs,
once in a blue moon, in his sleep.

1726

He names his days in descending order,
days left in a five-year sentence, calls them
by number as though they were years:

seventeen twenty-six
                    Dear Gracie I been
here a hundred years and still can't tell
you why I   He reflects a moment, pulls

the page loose, and proceeds.
                              Dear
Gracie anything I might say after these
hundred days would be just like   He bends

unconvinced to retrieve the dropped pencil
when my old man would make me read
the Bible, Adam begat Cain and Cain

Abel and so forth   He shakes
his head slowly, tells himself again
that words are hopeless, stretches

his fingers, writes
                    Dear Gracie it's
hard to start this letter so I'll begin
with now and circle back to explanations

1722

They say the captain sent our steers
to slaughter long since   Mose concentrates
briefly on the drip of the lavatory,

blunt end of the pencil against his lip
but all we've seen for meat is more
rabbit.
        They say we deserve a share

of what we helped raise   He suppresses
a doubt that scales his spine and presses
the pencil lead harder into the page

but they say it low. You may not
believe it but there are worse places
you can still disappear to if you raise

much hell   He surrenders, at last,
to self-intrigue, reviews the lines,
and reconvenes his misgivings:

But I know you may not see.
                Maybe
I don't know what I mean.
                They say
you can get worms if you eat bad rabbit

1719

Mose, in a white corridor, faces the wall
at the end of the row of white-
clad convicts facing the wall, waiting

for the current mandatory encounter
with the state's white-frocked nut doctor,
the guard in gray behind them slouching

against the opposite wall. Mose recalls
the last time he stood here, shifting
his weight to one foot and the other,

the line shifting, as now, every half
hour, across the salt-and-pepper tiles,
inching toward the unpainted metal door—

screws up his face as he remembers
being sent, unanalyzed, back to the peanut field,
"psychiatrist overloaded," Mose riding

alone but for the trusty at the wheel of the bus
and the sunbeams in diagonal shafts
through the steel cage, and the woman.

1710

A slight blond woman in a turquoise blouse
standing in a field of blue flowers, index
fingers linked before her cornflower skirt,

Gracie in bluebonnets, a picture of blue,
Mose in his place on the concrete floor,
back against the white cot, feet

by the round vertical bars, the snap-
shot resting on his knee in the faint
shadow of one of the square horizontal

bars: *I always write to your picture, Gracie,*
remember the one I took of you that time
we went down to Kerrville. Sometimes

I think it's really you and I'm really
talking not writing. Only I know.
And this letter ain't much account I know

but the thing would be if you could
come down or at least drop me a line.
I know I was wrong. Much love Mose.

1703

Dear Gracie, I'll go on and start over
writing you even when I know you
ain't had time to answer and maybe

the censors cut my letter up so you can't
hardly see what it says. And maybe
you don't feel like reading right now

He puts the pencil down and takes
a long drag on his cigarette, reflects
on the remaining light, and changes his mind:

It's hard to write you and I need my head
start. It's funny how people will want
something and when the time comes they

can't do it—my daddy would always
preach the mind of a man is desperately
wicked. So I don't know. I can tell you

one thing though, that is the human
is cagey and you got to be careful with him.
It's even the best that are

1702

more cagier even.
         Not just here either,
freeworlders too. Just like when I got
saved when I was six because they

say if you ask Jesus in you won't die
the second death and I was scared
to death of hell and so I went down

to the front of the church with everybody
singing Oh Lamb of God and prayed
and cried and they all gave me the right

hand of Christian fellowship. But the next
day it was just Monday and I was just
myself. Only I knew they expected something

new, so I swore on the Bible I'd be good,
but phony is just phony. That's how
I can always spot a fake now, I

was one. That's how come I don't hate
them too bad, because I was there before I
knew it, a sad excuse for a child or anyone.

1695

In the slow, dim moment before sleep,
he hears the blast of the siren-whistle,
third night in a row, lights

coming on suddenly, fiercely white, Gracie's
face hanging in each of the successive
blue spots before his eyes, the guard's

loud drawl as the siren dies: "All right
gentlemen, it's time to stand up and be
counted."
        Mose slides off the cot,

snakes himself up by the bars, rocks
on his heels as the footsteps approach,
the captain walking quickly down

the corridor tapping each cell door
with his stick, Mose blinking
at every tap, blue spots

dissolving into white and shadow
on white, the captain passing,
muttering "fifty-seven."

1694

They will tell you I got off easy, the deal
my lawyer made and the overcrowding
and all putting me here instead of Eastham

where it's real bad. But you got to count up
this easy and see what it equals, five
years with people that might stab you

over a pack of filter smokes unless they
figure you're so mean or crazy that for half
a pack plain you'd do them worse. Five

years instead of fifteen. In the free world
it's hard to see that the first hundred days
mostly decides if you die here, if you last out

after that they say It's just time. And time
like as not makes you worse instead of better,
at least I ain't never heard of nobody

setting here until one day they got
innocent.
        Not unless it was a dead
one maybe, and not lately at that.

1682

Well Gracie I have rambled on long
enough, but please write me because
even if I deserve to be here, I still don't

like it, it's still bad, and hearing from you
might keep me   The darkness appears,
the glow of the cherry on his cigarette

appears, and he moves its light close
and then away, as though it were a wand
he made to hover in the air. "Put

that cig out, Preacher." A voice
at the door.
             He takes a last drag
and, without getting up, flips the smoke

the sixteen inches to the toilet.
                   He hears
the short hiss and waits as long as he can
before exhaling the invisible smoke.

He closes without a light:

much love

mose

1680

He folds the letter in half and the half
in thirds, addresses the white envelope,
and, since light remains, begins again:

Dear Gracie I am hopefully awaiting
to hear from you so I will take the time
to write you meanwhile what I've seen

from the inside.
                For a while, they had us
in the McLennan County Jail. But one day they come
and fastened our hands and stuck a bunch of us

on this white schoolbus with steel screens
where it ought to have windows. It was ten
March and it was Waco, getting pretty

hot already, maybe 85 or so, I know
because going down Brazos River Drive
we all felt like hell, headed for the pen,

real quiet until somebody in the back said, "It's
spring." Because we could smell the mud
the rain and the river had washed down.

1678

The first few little things that happened
when we got off the bus and got here we were
pretty used to, they cut off our hair and took our

pictures. But then they gave us this manual
so we could read what they can do to you if you
don't tow under.
         It's supposed to be expired, but

He pauses, remembering the stiffness
in his neck that first night in his cell,
the cold feeling he had the next morning
         Prisoners

who cannot be made to observe the rules
may be punished by whipping with the strap
with such number of lashes, not exceeding twenty,

as may be authorized by the officer in charge
The light disappears and Gracie's face
rises in the darkness, blank,

expressionless, hollow
         Utmost care must be used
not to break the skin, and if the skin is broken
no further lashes shall be administered.

1674

Before we knew it they had us outside
the fence, cutting brush by a farm-
to-market road, I was with the hoe squad

that had to dig up a patch of dead briars.
I had a pitchfork to pile up what they
rooted out and raked. But I was afraid

of the trusty on his horse, so I kept up too good
and there came a minute with nothing to throw
and I made the mistake of leaning

on the fork handle, that big trusty hollered,
Peterson, and cracked his bullwhip three
inches from my ear and I dodged and pitched

right onto that pile of stickers, face
first and he said, You better work you goddamn
stupid hick, and spurred away.

I got off them brambles and wiped the blood
off my arms, and the boss looked where I'd mashed
the pile down and said, Shit, heavy as a dead preacher.

1667

So they took to calling me Preacher. It's pretty
common for a nickname, kind of funny though
when you think, if they only

knew. But if it killed me I wouldn't
let them find it out now. You can't
let people think about things

just any old way, because you give them
the wrong little detail on yourself, let them
get ahold of your first name, say, and they'll

get together and start you down
a road that's too tight to turn around on.
So you got to stay ahead.   He pauses and reaches

for his cigarette papers, bends one
into a trough with thumb and forefinger,
glances at her photograph on the cot.   *On me*

I figure they made the right mark,
but they don't know it and that's good as wrong,
maybe better than even nothing

1660

Mose looks up as the gray- and purple-uniformed
turnkey locks him in for the night, half
an hour before lights out.
                    Standing on a barrel

or stool in one position shall not extend
for more than two hours at any one
time
        Gracie watches over

the turnkey's shoulder. Mose
can see the bricks of the opposite wall
through her cheekbones.
                    No dark cell

hereafter constructed shall be of dimensions
less than four by eight feet, not less than seven
feet high, with proper ventilation
                    Gracie, sometimes you're

like a ghost to me or someone who's gone,
only their perfume is still there somehow
and the smell can make you see them

unless things are right in their places
                    and shall
not be occupied by more than one prisoner
at a time
        Mose closes his eyes

1659

Gracie I wish I could explain everything
so you could see how I got myself
here and what I was thinking. But I'll

tell you something—I can't tell you
the truth of what happened because one time
I remember it one way and another time

another. It's the same as that night
in bed I thought God was trying to tell me
to be a preacher. It was like the air

changed and made hair stand up
on my neck. And then a cloud came
over my face and I heard a goat

and a voice said, Mose feed the flocks. Or
at least that's the way I used to think
it was, that's what I used to tell people,

but now it seems like it was only the radio,
and the wind blowing the curtains out full,
and I was sleepy and kind of cold.

1655

Under a shower pipe Mose turns
as the sound of the boss's drawl pierces
the sound of water going down the hole

in the middle of the concrete room:
"Let's go, boys."
        Gracie in a white dress
stands near the guard, her back to the one

showerless wall, the doorway dark
between them. Mose stares, water
pounding his neck and shoulders as he leans

one way and the other to keep her
in sight over the intervening bodies
of men beginning to leave—
        "Let's move,

Preacher"—
        her eyes half closed, her mouth a thin
straight line high on her face, as though she squinted
at the sun or something distasteful.
        "Peterson

get your ugly ass out."
        When he turns
full face to the boss, he hears the faint rustle,
knows without looking she is gone.

1650

I've thought a lot on how I landed
up in here. Mostly you can't make sense
out of it, like why didn't I stop

myself before I done it. I
don't know.
               I'm not trying to get out
of it, Gracie, I deserve being here,

but not because I decided to do it
just right out of a blue sky. Actual reasons,
I didn't have none, and when things started,

it was like playing, I never meant it
to turn real. But it was already
headed for real before I was ready and I

thought to myself, Now it's too late.
                              It makes
me think there's another world underneath
this one and everything there is backwards

to what we want. I know I'm not in this hole
for having pimples on my face
but it seems like most things start up down there

where it's dark and slick and no handholds anywhere

1643

Gracie I've waited all this time and never
a word from you
> He hears the sound
of her dress in the corridor, closes

his eyes, tells himself he doesn't believe.
The cell door slides in its track, open
then shut
> It ain't real
> > He feels the cot

give, someone sitting down next to him.
> > > > This whole
thing is phony, she's been writing me all
along only somebody has got it away, always

somebody taking something or keeping you
from seeing what's yours
> > He thinks
of a cigarette and his eyes open. Gracie

sits inches from him; he resists the impulse
to touch her, simply looks, anticipating sudden
darkness, at her hands skirted in lace

and folded in her lap, her blond hair draped
over one shoulder, the long sleeved white
gown, her eyes unmoving, blank and blue.

1640

"Peterson!" barks the big trusty.
                Mose's
blood sings, first in memory of the bullwhip,
then with the dumb joy of hearing his name

read, finally, at dinner mail call.
Gracie in her white dress walks
over tabletops, over the air

between tables, sits down on Mose's table,
her feet on an empty chair, knees
at his elbow. She extends the letter.

He tears open the censor's brown envelope. The pale
green stationery crawls with the curly
letters of Gracie's hand   *Dear Mose*

He trembles and looks away, fumbling
for a cigarette.
              Dear Mose I
                    He sees her
hips through the paper, the formica

tabletop through her hips. The page
disappears between his hands. Somebody
jostles him getting up to leave.

1639

What would she have said?
              At three
o'clock in the dark, bleary-eyed, Mose
rehearses probabilities:
                    Dearest

Criminal, how do you like it now   no
she's way above that
                    Listen Mose
I won't bother to   He turns over

onto his stomach, listens to his heart
beating in the cot frame. Far down
the hallway somewhere bars slide shut.

Mose how could you betray me so
if you loved me why did
you
        He presses his forehead to the wall

closes his eyes tightly, exhales. The pulsing
white lines inside his eyelids solidify,
gather slowly, as if they were merely mist,

curve and swirl, an outline of Gracie,
arms crossed in front of her, her
chin pointing down toward her shoulder.

1639

Mose in the frisk line, half asleep,
waits his turn to be cleared and counted
and to climb the three steps, to enter

the steel cage, to find his seat on the bus
and wait. To ride again to the peanut field,
to wrestle again with the shovel

and the boss and the trusty, to write
Gracie. Again. His eyelids flutter, he nods
and jerks, almost tripping into the white

back in front of him. He twists one shoulder
toward the other and stretches his neck.
                                              Dear
Mose you are not   He raises both hands

over his head; one guard slaps at arm-
pits, ribs, belly, hips, while another runs
his hands up Mose's right leg, down his left.

Gracie please I know I can't expect   *Dear*
Mose you put me
                          "Move," says the guard.
                                              Mose's
feet, like distant stones, stumble forward.

1639

The apprehension that he is falling: he tenses
his shoulders, his stomach
shrinks, a waking reflex

kicks the steel leg of the bus seat, the sun glazes
over the morning like a dead
man's eye

in the clouds. Gracie hovers, brooding
everywhere, invisible and certain,
a haze

in the tips of tall weeds that streak now
and then past the window, the pale day-moon
speared on a fence

post, Mose still
clawing through his *Dear
Gracie how am I*

*going to do the rest of this
time in
between?*

1629

Mose awakens the invisible turnkey
turns his lock the cell door
slides like some voice

slowly urging Come

on Preacher Mose paces

down the corridor bars and anonymous

faces remote
controlled
doors shuddering groaning metal

tracks Mose clenches his

teeth

facing the barbarically

brilliant central Texas midday wonders
why he wonders what time
it is metallic noise the barb

laden outer gate rolls back on tires a door in the sun

opens when Mose reaches

the horizon

White roaring
door into the glaring river
where

angels two by deafening

two

with glass shovels stand

light raging between bones in their black
flame wings
that same shade as before was their

portal

perspiration on his white fatigues a shining
pulpit rises he throws
down his
cigarette

a voice like the sun's
trumpet
      Mose

take care of

my

lambs

engraved on the altar ablaze **Mose**

take care

you feed these poor sheep he
steps up clears his throat *Beloved*
the black word from his mouth rapidly
recedes into the glowing

distance
           In
the beginning was the word male
and female created he words

flying away darkly into the deep

blinding

air
    Men shall be given water
all they can drink and two
pieces of bread
                  letters line the fierce sky a black lace

gown *my love thy breasts are lilies beneath*
thy belly a heap of
wheat
        poor sinner inside the sun

I thought

it would be

quiet

and God called the day good

and the darkness called he

light the fire dome's

net of words

beginning slowly to turn *No solitary*

occupant shall be handcuffed or

shackled howling

rows of words

whirling around the celestial

hemisphere

horizon to zenith

roaring *oh*

my love where

do you keep your

flocks?

He falls forward, barely
catches himself, the white

surface swallows his hands, he
twists, sits flat on the ground, dizzy

legs crooked in front of him, snow
soaking through his fatigues. Grey block

letters on a drift say **Peterson**, it is not
snow either, it is his shirt
hung on a chair by the corrugated

steel trough of cold water he floats in.
                                        The trusty
orderly holds out a thermometer—Mose
takes it under his tongue, stares at the black

bars of the infirmary.
                        "You'll be
all right once your pressure comes up,
heatstroke ain't nothing. Captain's got you

down for sick call tomorrow."
                                        Mose
exhales, feels his torso decline into the water,
tightens and relaxes his grip on the gray tub's edge.

1623

He awakens: the same low light
washes the white windowless
expanse of room, same **Prohibido**

Fumar/No Smoking sign on the wall,
thin infirmary bars, black letters **Prop**
TDC on the hem of the bed sheet. He stares

at the ceiling, fingers laced together
behind his neck, elbows on the pillow
corners   *Dear Gracie, In this place*

you can't tell night and day, you
wake up and time starts off right
where it was before. If I could look

in a mirror, I think I'd see something shine
like animal eyes in the dark.
When the headlights round a curve,

it ain't a possum, skunk,
or armadillo, they're like the same,
just a there that don't know what to think.

1622

"Peterson!"
                Dog-eyed Mose looks up
from his dinner tray, unable
to feel any chill in his back, anything

beyond the slight apprehension trailing away
like wisps from the end of a cigarette.
                                        The manila
envelope hangs from the trusty's thumb and finger.

Mose rises, his hand rises like a piece
of machinery, he watches himself take the package,
return to his tray, reposition himself on his stool,

absent, empty.
                He shakes his head
very slightly, as though to himself. Mail. He has
a large brown envelope. He takes his tray

to the track, the fatigue of a first
day back in the peanut fields crawling
up the backs of his legs. He returns

to his cell, sits down, dumps the envelope
onto his bed:
                tattered sheets
of newspaper.
                He blinks once and lies down.

1621

He dreams he is sleeping with a brick
under his shoulder, a numb fire
in his fingers, his elbow flickering

going out:
        he stirs, strains
against the weight of his own arm,
gives up, and turns over toward it.
                He is not asleep,

the brick is small, made of metal, a jack-
knife he thinks. No. Too light,
a grid on one side.
        He lies still, lifts it

to his lips, draws softly, hears
the four-note chord in the dark.
            The newspaper
was only the wrapping it dropped out of.

He thinks of the harmonica passing censors,
trusties eager to steal anything available,
any comfort at anyone's expense: he thinks

he must not be awake, must be
losing himself again, but his arm still tingles
as though it were marched over by ants.

1620

It *had* to be.
            He sits on the cot, his head
clearing for the first time in days.
                           Gracie
I can't figure if it was you sent me this

harmonica, don't know why if it was.
I've seen men get killed
over such. Why didn't you write
                       He picks up

the envelope: no return address, his name typed.
He inspects the postmark: a circle of 27
September Waco T X
                It *could* be. He pulls out

the newspaper and thumbs through, seeking
the slight hint: a crossword worked in her
peculiar hand, the barb on the hook of its **t,**

its **i** dotted with a tiny circle; perhaps
a classified circled in red scrawl, a marginal
pencil scribble with smudged fingerprint,

or a strand of blond hair caught on the ragged
edge of a page. A blue fiber from her dress maybe,
or a stray mark of lipstick, her color.

1619

The brown mark from a coffee cup's bottom
draws his eye to the photograph:
his own face staring back, as through a dark

quarter moon, from a small square in an inside
leaf of the paper, his name captioned,
the headline
        SUSPECT APPREHENDED.
            He blows

lightly on the harmonica, a single short
burst of chord like an accident. His eye
drifts down the column's right margin

              deputies arrested
            death of a woman in
       Peterson after a protracted

             help of Waco's K-9
        "We pursued the individual
     whereabouts when an anonymous

            FOR LIVESTOCK PRICES

              decline in hog

He draws a breath; the harmonica drones.

1618

He tears his picture from the paper—coffee
mark scoring his face like an enormous
mustache—and holds it next to the photo

of Gracie from his wallet: the contrast of her color
to his black-and-white making him feel
like a shadow. He feels beneath the bedrail, pulls up

a wad of chewing gum and fixes the pictures
to the cinderblocks   *Gracie I'm hanging*
both of our pictures up side by side

just trying to get them out of my head
and onto the wall. It's funny
how something can be a man's life

and salvation for so long, like carrying
your picture was to me, and then one day
something seems off, you have to move

things around, it's changed.   He looks
at the photos: between them, on the torn
edge of the newspaper, he has left the letter "c."

1616

Dear Gracie I have always loved you ever
since we was both little kids,
that's why it like to killed me

when your mama and my old man
married, all I could think was he finally
got her away from me. He knew I couldn't

have you if you was my sister or he'd spring
some unknown Bible verse on me and make
me out a big sinner just like always, therefore

did God give them over to their own
lusts, henceforth did God harden
their hearts that they might not

hear and all. He used to say you
was a pearl of great price and I wasn't
nothing more than just a swine bound

and determined to ruin and trample you, I'd
never amount to nothing. You're just Ichabod,
he'd say, which means God's glory has fled.

1605

I reckon they have told you how I am
the lowest excuse for a slimy dog
that ever was
            He puts the harmonica

to his lips, picks out a slow, jerky
version of the song in his mind
                          I will change
out of this mortal clay
                 but I'm still here

hoping to hear something from you,
holding out longer and longer all
in a place where that's dangerous, where it

makes it easier to get killed
                   and the midnight
will shine bright as day
                              but I
want you to hear how things happened, it ain't

like they have made out. I may not can
remember everything perfect, but I was
there, didn't dream all of it the way

the papers did
              O come gentle Lord
take me soon
take me soon

1604

It all begun the night of the revival, I had
set by that Linda girl on account of you was still
in Kerrville and she asked me. She was sweet

on me, maybe, judging how things come out
but she never had let on for years before. We walked
home, I can't even remember what we said

but when we got to her daddy's farm she looked
at me real sad and run off into the barn.
I went in there but it was too dark

so I groped back for the light. There was a harrow
laying there upside down, the tongue
was propped up on a block like somebody

was working on it. I said, Where are you Linda,
because I couldn't see her nowhere, and she said, Come
up Mose, and I looked where her voice had been, high

up in the hayloft. Only I didn't see her, I just saw
the tail of her lavender dress hanging
off the edge where she had threw it on the hay.

1603

He turns through the newspaper: it is **not**
one newspaper, but a collection of leaves
from different papers folded together—

a March Waco Tribune-Herald sheet
enclosing pages of endless other dates
and names, Lorena Examiner Weekly, Whitney

Post-Historian, Gatesville American.
                                        LOCAL MAN
SOUGHT IN DEATH   His face hardens, he breathes
through his teeth, and looks to her picture:

colored paper like a face on his wall
                                        SENTENCE
SET FOR MINISTER'S SON   He refolds the paper slowly,
tightly, and throws it against the wall. It flutters

and falls in a heap by the toilet
                                        BRUTAL
MURDER LEAVES TOWN FEARFUL
                                        He presses
his lips together, relaxes his shoulders,

looks first at his feet on the gray floor,
then at the harsh light over his head,
mutters to himself, Go out. Go out.

1602

I never done anything like that and never
ought to have went up that ladder, I took
ahold of her but I hadn't no sooner

thought of you than the shame hit me, she
put me in mind of some hunching dog and I couldn't
go it no more. I tried not to let on in my face

but she could tell and she slapped me
and pulled hair and hollered like a cat, Your sister's
between us, ain't she? Step-

sister, I tried to say but she scratched me
and said I'll tell you what the whole town
knows, it's your damned old man your sweet

Gracie lays down for and right under your big
stupid nose too.
                    I hit her hard, right

in the eye before I even thought
and she went down backwards over a bale
off the edge of the loft, down
where them harrow teeth was waiting on her.

1601

He spreads the papers on his cot's white sheets,
his name in the headline like a reflection
of the name on the front of his shirt.
                                        PETERSON

ADMITS GUILT
           it's your damned old man
                              the confessed
killer showed no emotion   your sweet Gracie
lays down for   **as he entered the plea**   I'll tell

you what the whole town knows   **an anonymous**
source confirmed   a pearl of great   **appeared**
to have been subsequently beaten   just a swine

bound and determined   **Times and Review reporters**
have learned   right under your big stupid
nose   **from a hayloft onto a pile**

of farm implements   it couldn't be
true what she said, she was
trying to make me mad, that was all

lies, all of it was a god-damn
                        The light
goes softly out. He pulls off his dirty canvas
shoes and sets them quietly on the concrete floor.

1600

By the time I'd got down and pulled her up
off them spikes her eyes was already staring,
I thought, I've got to go get somebody,

only I looked back at her laying there in blood
naked and hay in her hair and her mouth
wide open, eyes aiming straight up and I thought

how my old man always said I was a son of
perdition and I told myself, You must have
egged her on some way, you must have wanted this

in your true heart, You can't go back now,
not with her eye making a shiner
where you hit her, not when them big trials

will find the skin and hair under
the woman's nails and that proves it,
so that's why I run off to Waco. It

didn't do no good, they caught me anyway,
I shouldn't never have done it, shouldn't never
have played along or been there at all.

1599

All that long drive to Waco I was praying to God
it would be a dream in the end, but I knew
it never is a dream when it's that way.   He puffs

on the harmonica, the song moving too slowly
                                        When I go
to that eternal
                It was real dark, no
moon yet, I was gunning it down the back roads

thinking How am I going to live now that I
have killed a person?
                        the bride
and wife of the Lamb
                        I saw some headlights once

or twice, way off, and I wondered if they was
coming after me, if anyone had called the law yet,
or if anyone besides me had seen her,
                                O the joy

I will feel in that city
                        but they all turned off
the road before we met or else just passed by
regular. It was hot but I had my windows

rolled up, I was shivering, waiting for the patrol
car that would turn around and follow me
                                        When I
open my eyes to the light

1598

I don't know as I even thought I'd make it
to Waco, I didn't have no plan in mind
when I got there anyway. I got worried

because I kept thinking, They'll know me
by my car, that's how they catch you, by make
and model and the numbers on your plate, they talk

on radios and that's how they all know. I left
the Ford southeast of town and walked up the Brazos.
I was shaking and I said out loud, Where am I

headed, and my mind kind of said back, Cameron
Park, way back in the woods where numbers can't
help them, you can get a chance to rest up and

figure. I felt better then, it was strange that I
could. But it was nice to walk at night, right between
that thin black river and the lights of town

all hazy and it was getting late and lonesome,
nobody on the streets, just the sound of water
and me passing them long rows of streetlights.

1597

I was okay until I got to the graveyard,
that old one, you know, where all the Texas
Rangers was buried
He pauses and puts down

the pencil, looks at the headstones beyond the iron
spikes of the fence, the large tangle of crape
myrtle pressing up from the riverbank, the magnolia

towering at the corner of the railing, its broad
leaves absolutely still in the heavy, humid night.
He stops, hands in his pockets:
I bet they had

found her already, something had told
somebody, Go out and look in that barn. Maybe
there really are ghosts in the world,

but they always stay right behind you,
you never see them, but they know
how to put things in your head. I guessed

that all them Rangers would follow me, somehow
they would know I done it.
He breathes faster
and goes up the road, running hard.

1596

A dog still barks far behind him, Mose
among dark saplings
wheezes, wonders

why he ran in the night air, the stick
he steps on cracks like an fragile
spine, he feels he is

being watched, looks quickly over his shoulder:
no one there, he licks
his dry lips.
          Something moves

under the leaves, Mose moves past granite
outcroppings, the terrain becomes rugged,
grandaddy

longlegs scurries over a rotted log in the moonlight,
a man in a white dress shirt face down
in the humus,

covered with scorpions, no, it is only
trash from a picnic, Mose breathes
hard again and keeps walking.

The light creeps up in the east, the river waits
far below the bluff, heavy-eyed Mose
stares

over the edge   **The Spirit and the Bride say**
Come   the sky buzzes, he laces
his fingers

through his hair   **Come ye blessed**
of the Father   and of the
woman for-

ever and ever and of the beautiful blue
figures coming toward him along the cliff   **Who**
are these arrayed thus   blue

uniforms,
two police dogs, Mose scrambles
back from the edge, runs down the hill   **The heavens**
shall roll up like a scroll   the growling

and crashing in the brush behind him, he feels
the chill under his ribs   **Then**
shall the noontime turn

black as sackcloth   the faceless
coin
cartwheels across the sky

rolling up his time on its
windlass, he runs through nettles   **Let him**
that is athirst come   through thorns

slashing his arms   **It is finished it is**
done   eyes peer from the rocks,
the lichens

speak   **The hour not even the angels**
know   hands reach from the ground,
claws scratch at his

heels, his chest heaves, the sweet
odor of blood,
the dragon,

the dragon   **I am crucified**
with Christ

The dogs bring him down.

The whirr of handcuffs and the barking
of dogs become the noise of the cellblock,
men's voices and clanging bars
                              Gracie, I know I'm no

good from your way of seeing things, but I got
my own way. Mainly, I set in the county
jail and waited on you or my old man to go

my bail, nobody but a lawyer would even talk
to me and they made him do it. And I set
in the courthouse by myself while the big

shots argued about me, and I been setting
in this hole now for eight months,
all the time waiting for a sign from you,

anything at all, and you ain't throwed me
even a crumb, not even a Dear
John I'm in love with your Daddy, not

even nothing.
                    If you think I'm the very
devil, it looks like you could still write
and tell me so.   Yours, Mose.

1595

He reviews the previous week's
scrawl—his words remind him of the hymn
and it plays over and over in his head:

**There is a fountain filled with blood
drawn from Emmanuel's veins**   I ain't writing
no more if she don't
                  He takes the harmonica

from his pocket, brings it to his face   **There
is a fountain filled**   it ain't
no use, ain't no one listening

anyway   **filled with blood**   She'll toss it
straight in the fire or put it in a shoebox
in some dark closet, won't even read it.

He takes her photograph down from the wall,
pulls his own picture down with it, folds
them both inside the letter, and crumples it all

into a yellow wad. He stares at the toilet,
the dripping wash basin, the white
cinderblock walls, the bars.

1594

Well Gracie, the peanuts are in, the wind
come up out of the north this morning,
there was a shower in the forenoon.

                              I'm over Indian

summer I reckon. They say we don't work
much outside when it's chilly and damp, they say
everything slows up as the temperature

drops
        He thinks of the harmonica, reaches
instead into the other pocket for his cigarette
pack
        They call it good sleeping weather,

sounds to me like it'll just make sleep
harder come by around here.
                              He lights
his smoke and props his feet on the rim

of the toilet.
                The harp will help
if I don't get killed over it, maybe I won't,
I play it real soft. But I still need

a letter from you Gracie, because we don't
know who'll make it around to spring
again, and you know how winter is, usually

just a long cold spell with rain.

University Press of New England publishes books under its own imprint and is the publisher for Brandeis University Press, Brown University Press, University of Connecticut, Dartmouth College, Middlebury College Press, University of New Hampshire, University of Rhode Island, Tufts University, University of Vermont, Wesleyan University Press, and Salzburg Seminar.

About the Author
Loren Graham was born in Broken Arrow, Oklahoma in 1958. He attended college in Oklahoma and Texas and afterwards worked for some time as a teacher in a private high school in Waco and as an English instructor in the Texas penitentiary system. In 1988, he took his M.F.A. from the University of Virginia. He is now Assistant Professor of English at Lynchburg College in Virginia.

Library of Congress Cataloging-in-Publication Data
Graham, Loren, 1958–
    Mose / Loren Graham.
        p.   cm. — (Wesleyan poetry)
    ISBN 0–8195–2215–5. — ISBN 0–8195–1220–6 (pbk.)
    I. Title.   II. Series.
    PS3557.R2154M67   1994
    811'.54—dc20   94–15412
    ∞